BIG JOURNEY
OF LITTLE BUNNY

Children picture book about Bunny adventure for ages 3-8
Copyright © 2023 by Ira Martur

On Christmas Eve Bunny woke up earlier than usual.
Today he was going to leave the woods for the first time ever to go to the city, to buy a Christmas gift for his sister Varya.

This was his big secret, not even Mummy and Daddy knew. Bunny had been planning his trip for a long time and was not afraid…mostly.
Wasting no time at all, he put his money, a piece of apple pie and a flashlight into his little bag, put on his hat and determinedly left the house.

Mr. Bullfinch was sitting in his usual place near cottage. It seemed to Bunny that Mr. Bullfinch was always busy with very serious thoughts. Bunny crumbled some of the apple pie on the snow and called Mr. Bullfinch.
When Mr. Bullfinch had finished pecking all the crumbs, Bunny asked: "Can you please fly up high and show me which way the city is?"

Mr. Bullfinch nodded, flapped his wings, and in a moment was on top of the tallest pine, pointing the direction with his wing. Bunny thanked Mr. Bullfinch and set off.

Bunny walked and walked and after a while came to a clearing in the woods. A very tall man in a hat stood there looking far into the distance.
"Sir, how far it is to the city?" asked Bunny. But the tall man didn't even move.
"Excuse me…," Bunny said again, coming closer…

"He will not answer you," said Squirrel in the tree above, "this is a snowman made by the city kids; and the city is right behind those trees."
Bunny laughed, waved to Squirrel and hurried off to the city.

"Uh-oh…," thought Bunny, once on the city street. Everything around was noisy, buzzing and rushing at great speed. Bunny did not dare to move.
"Are you lost, little one?" he heard from a voice nearby. It was a big dog with a red collar.
"Can you tell me how to get to the store?" asked Bunny bravely.
"Let me give you a lift," Dog offered, "climb up on my back or else you will be trampled on!"
And Dog walked down the street with Bunny on his back.

Near the entrance to the store Dog stopped.
"Now you can go in on your own, there are cats in there," said Dog, grimacing.
"Thank you very much," Bunny said, as he headed into the store. It was warm in the store and yes, there were two dozing cats, one black and one white. Also there were so many other things that Bunny started get confused.

"There is a toy store opposite," White Cat purred, opening just one eye.
"I don't need toys; I need a real necklace!" Bunny replied sounding confident.
"What a funny bunny," said Black Cat while doing the biggest stretch, "let's help him."

So, the cats, who knew everything in the store, helped Bunny to choose the most beautiful necklace.
And even packed it into a gift box with a big shiny ribbon.

On the way back Bunny was very pleased with himself. He knew the way home now, and the job was done. Bunny hopped merrily, clutching his bag with the gift in his little paws.

Soon Bunny saw familiar trees and the snowman. Bunny jumped even faster, but suddenly the snowman moved and it turned out that it was not a snowman at all, but a big, huge bear! It was too late to hide and Bunny just froze and closed his eyes.

"Who's trembling here?" asked Bear, approaching and sniffing.
"Don't eat me, I don't taste very nice," said Bunny without opening his eyes.

"I don't eat bunnies,
I love honey,"
Bear reassured him.
"Let me take you home,
it will be getting dark soon."
And Bear quickly walked through
the woods with Bunny in his paws.

Once at home, Bunny safely put his gift under the Christmas tree for Varya to open on Christmas Day.
"Wow! What a surprise!" Mummy, Daddy and Varya exclaimed when Bunny pulled out his gift.
They could not even imagine how and where Bunny got it from.

And Bunny then opened the presents from his family, which were a toy truck and a toy dinosaur.

Bunny also received four more surprise gifts.
Who do you think they were from?

Here is a special place for your ideas -
write or draw them here

Bunny made the map of his big journey.

Meet Ira, the author of the brave Bunny book series and the proud mom of two little bunnies who just happen to be the stars of her books.

Sometimes these bunnies aren't the most well-behaved, but they sure are funny and their antics make for great stories! With more tales to come, young readers can't wait to see what kind of trouble these bunnies will get into next.

If you know who brought four surprise gifts for Bunny, share your answer HERE and receive Maze from Bunny!

linktr.ee/ira_martur

Your voice truly matters. So, if you enjoyed this book, your heartfelt review is very much appreciated and so very important.
Please take a minute to leave it HERE.
Thank you!

Did you know that…
Bunnies can hop for very long distances.
They can make a jump that is 10 times their own length.
Imagine being able to jump over a bus!

All rights reserved. Thank you for buying an authorised addition of this book and for complying with copyright laws by not reproducing any part of this book with our written permission.

Printed in the USA
CPSIA information can be obtained
at www.ICGtesting.com
LVHW061908171123
764118LV00019B/1095

9 788396 915009